# Father to Daughter

# Father

## to

# Daughter

### Life Lessons on
### Raising a Girl

Harry H. Harrison Jr.

WORKMAN PUBLISHING COMPANY • NEW YORK

Library of Congress Cataloging-in-Publication Data

Harrison, Harry H.
  Father to daughter : life lessons on raising a girl / by Harry H.
Harrison Jr.
    p. cm.
  Rev. edition.
  ISBN 978-0-7611-7489-9 (alk. paper)
  1. Fathers and daughters. 2. Parenting. 3. Fatherhood. I. Title.
HQ755.85.H374 2013
306.874'2--dc23

                                              2012033128

Design by Janet Vicario
Illustrations by Matt Wawiorka

Workman books are available at special discounts when purchased in bulk
for premiums and sales promotions as well as for fund-raising or educational
use. Special editions or book excerpts can be created to specification.
For details, contact the Special Sales Director at the address below or
send an email to specialmarkets@workman.com.

Workman Publishing Company, Inc.
225 Varick Street
New York, NY 10014
workman.com
fearlessparenting.com

WORKMAN is a registered trademark of Workman Publishing Co., Inc.

Printed in the U.S.A.
First printing March 2013
10  9  8  7  6  5  4

# Preface

I was amazed and gratified by the response to my earlier book, *Father to Son*.

So many dads (and moms) of boys told me how much reading it meant to them. As an author, you treasure those moments.

But the most surprising thing was that dads of girls told me they read the book, too. I asked them, "Well, is raising a girl like raising a boy?" and mostly they'd smile and say, "No, it's another world."

And they'd ask why there wasn't a father book for them. With all the interest and sentiment devoted to the mother-daughter relationship, the relationship between fathers and daughters was often overlooked. But, of course, a strong, loving father is as important to a girl as he is to a boy.

So, spurred to action by several dear friends, I set out to interview dads of successful daughters. Their daughters are academic powerhouses, star athletes, talented artists, honors graduates, fearless missionaries, and successful entrepreneurs. These women embrace their roles as mothers and wives and breadwinners because of the way they were raised. These dads had obviously done an outstanding job. Their daughters are changing society. They had changed their dads.

All the men I interviewed shared one precept: that it was important to be involved in their daughters' lives.

This is really their book. I just wrote down what they said.

# Introduction

Raising a girl takes two parents:

A mom to show her how to be a woman.

A dad to encourage her to be fearless.

A dad's job is to make his daughter courageous. To make her feel beautiful. To give her a sense of adventure. To give her security and the confidence to handle any situation.

The relationship between a dad and a daughter is very simple: She will love her father and trust him completely, forever.

Because he's her first love. Her first hero. The first man in her life.

# The Five Keys

1. Always be involved in her life.

2. Respect and honor her mom.

3. Treasure every moment with her.

4. Pray for her every day.

5. Be her hero.

# The Wonder
# Years

Realize from the beginning that even at one week old, she's a girl. So she's going to be just as charming, and just as mystifying, as every other girl you know. Being her dad will not change this.

$A$ccept the fact that she will melt your heart anytime she chooses.

Take part in her life now. Don't wait until she's fifteen to try to develop a relationship.

She may look
adorable, but be
forewarned—her
diaper is going to be
just as challenging as
any boy's.

When you get home from work, hold her as much as possible. This is for your benefit as much as hers.

Sing to her while you're rocking her. She'll love hearing your voice—and it's a great way to pass the time at 1 a.m.

Be sure to take
a lot of photos of
her now. She is
changing every day.

Tell her from Day One that she can accomplish anything.

Let her sleep on
your chest when she's
a baby. This is when
the world begins to
make sense.

Yes, she's a girl. But her screams will be as loud as any baby boy's when she's hungry or tired or upset.

Make her part of your
world—let her see you shave,
work, read, and relax.
She'll love spending time
with you, no matter
what you're doing.
Enjoy it while it lasts.

Memorize her face.
Her eyes. Her hands.
She'll be memorizing
everything about you.

Keep saying "Daddy"
over and over to her.
There's a good chance
"Da-Da" will be her
first word.

Introduce her to the joys of ice cream and chocolate sauce. She'll have as much fun playing with it as she will eating it.

Give her baths.
Do not leave this
to Mom alone.
It is pure magic.

Come to grips with the
fact that you cannot
carry her around
all her life. She will
eventually have to
learn to walk.

Remember,
if you yell at a boy
not to play with
a wall socket,
he'll either stomp
off or do it anyway.
A girl will cry.

When she babbles at
you in baby talk, always
respond with a positive:
"Yes." "Of course."
"You're right." Soon
enough, you'll be telling
her "no" all the time.

Her mom will show her how to bake chocolate chip cookies. You show her how to dunk them in milk.

Realize when she starts walking that anything she can reach will disappear. Find a childproof place for your keys. Your cell phone. The TV remote.

Know that while you will never understand her thing for dolls, you will buy her more of them than you can possibly imagine.

Teach her to count.
First her fingers.
Then Cheerios, M&Ms,
dandelions, and
fireflies.

Emotionally, physically, and spiritually healthy girls are raised in a loving atmosphere. Do all you can to create a tranquil, harmonious home.

Let the family dog sit under her high chair at dinner. Your daughter will be a source of food for him, and the dog will be a constant source of wonder for her.

Invest money in a college fund. *Now.*

Be prepared
to watch Disney
movies with her
some 200 times.
Each.

Your wife can play
her Mozart and
Beethoven symphonies.
You introduce her to
the Beatles.

Tickle her,
play with her,
give her piggyback
rides. She's not
breakable.

Never abandon
the sense of wonder
that comes from
watching her and
her mother together.

Relish the moments when she toddles up and for no reason at all throws her arms around your neck. Resist the urge to buy her the world.

Trust her mom
to understand the
mystery of little
girls. You have yet
to figure out the
mystery of big ones.

Realize that if you take her on a plane trip before she can talk, there's a good chance she'll scream for two and a half hours.

# Encourage her to go barefoot.

# Never, ever make fun of her.

Bear in mind that from the very beginning, your personality will shape her.

Realize that as you shape her, she will shape you.

Don't think that because she's a sweet little girl she can't throw food with the best of them.

Buy her a beautiful necklace very early on. Continue to add pearls or precious stones to it as she grows older.

When you take her to the movies, be ready for her to bring along five or six of her favorite stuffed animals. When fathers of boys look at you strangely, act as if her behavior makes perfect sense.

She will want a pet.
She will also want
to dress her pet in
costumes and take it
for strolls in her doll
carriage.

Take her out shopping,
just the two of you.
Remember, she's five.
You don't need to
threaten your 401(k).
But you'll be tempted.

Always remember, she can do anything a boy can do. (In fact, her odds of going to medical school are better than a boy's!)

Brush her hair.
You'll be amazed
at how long she'll
want you to do this.

Never forget that fathers who aren't just supportive but also *around* produce daughters with high self-esteem.

Read to her often.
Very soon, she'll be
reading to you.

Build a shelf for her dolls and stuffed animal collection. Ask her to tell you stories about each one.

Have tea parties with her. Nibble on whatever she puts in front of you. Tell her it's delicious.

Take her to
the zoo. She'll love
the elephants,
the monkeys, the lions,
the petting zoo—
everything.

Buy her a jungle gym. However, if she falls off that jungle gym, disregard those thoughts about killing yourself.

Encourage her to
play with the boys.
Nicely.

Take her fishing.
She'll be disgusted
by the worm on
the hook, but she'll
love reeling in
the fish.

Play catch with her.
Even if the ball is pink
and covered with
glitter.

Talk to her about what she wants to be when she grows up. Continually reinforce the idea that anything is possible.

Don't tolerate her
temper tantrums.
Not now. Not when
she's fifteen.
Your home will be
more peaceful for this.

Restrict her
TV viewing, unless
you want her to grow
up with the values
Hollywood teaches.

Dance with
her always.
She'll never be
too young.
Or too old.

Remember, if a little girl doesn't get a nap, she can resemble something from a Stephen King novel.

Put galoshes on her and take her out to stomp in mud puddles.

Little girls
are fascinated
by escalators.
Make sure you hold
her hand.

# Make her a Valentine's Day card—every year.

Take her
horseback riding.
Girls *love* horses.

Lie on your backs in the grass and look for shapes in the clouds together. It's a good way to approach life when you're young.

You'll notice that little girls love to have their faces painted with rainbows and stars. Be prepared to have several rainbows painted on *your* face every now and then, too.

Be home for dinner on time. This is very important.

Believe it or not, when she's two and a half, she's ready for a bike with training wheels. You, however, might not be.

Ask her about
her day, every day.
Share her wonder.

Keep her secrets.
This way she will
begin to trust men.

Write this down:
Girls cry. A lot.

Sure, give her a
baseball glove for
her birthday.
Or a hockey stick.

Little girls love
a hose and a sandbox.
They also love to rip off
their clothes after they
get them wet.
Don't freak out.

Take her for a walk in the woods. Show her what poison ivy looks like, how to cross a stream, how to find her way back.

Let her teach you about what she learned today. About the Pilgrims or multiplication or manatees. How to sing her favorite song. How to bake a cake. How to braid Barbie's hair.

Show her how to play poker. It involves math, bluffing, paying attention, taking risks, making decisions, and knowing when to fold 'em and move on.

Resist the urge to let her sleep in your bed when she's scared or sick. Independence starts in childhood. So sit with her in her own room until she falls back to sleep.

Teach her not to be afraid of boys, but to be ready to challenge them.

When she's old enough, sign her up for karate lessons. This is more for your sake than hers.

Plant flowers with her. Even if your garden is on a windowsill.

**D**on't be surprised if
during her first sleepover
she calls you at 3 a.m.
to come pick her up.
The fact that she misses
you is a wonderful thing.

She will fall in love
with dogs, kittens,
birds, and stuffed
unicorns. It may make
no sense to you.
Just smile.

If another girl or boy hurts her in any way, you will feel a very real inclination to inflict harm. Resist it. This impulse won't get any weaker as your daughter gets older.

Show her how to climb a tree. Also how to climb down.

Praise her often.
Let her know you love
her the way she is.
If you tell her this often
enough, she might
remember it throughout
adolescence.

Make up stories to tell each other at night. Stretch her imagination.

Remember, little sisters
will idolize, chase, and
annoy their big brothers
and sisters all through
those brothers' and
sisters' teenage years.
It's really no one's fault.

Teach her how and
when to call 911.

Unleash her on a computer when she's four and she may be writing code by the time she's eight.

Learn to read her moods. The day is coming when she won't talk about everything with you.

Buy her
a chemistry set.
Tell her it would be
nice if her experiments
didn't involve smoke,
fire, or her little
brother.

Get involved at her school. Go to the PTA meetings. Meet her teachers. Know what's going on.

Encourage her to try
new things while she's
young, and she'll be
more willing to try
new things when
she's older.

Teach her it's more important to show off her brains than her body.

Surprise her by showing up at her school for lunch, bearing Happy Meals or pizza.

Always respect
her privacy.
And modesty.

Don't pry into the stories she and her mother tell each other. They'll let you in on them when they want to.

Read her stories from your local newspaper or *The New York Times* or *Wall Street Journal* websites. This will spark a lifelong habit.

Teach her computer safety early on. That chatting with friends is fun but she should never, ever, ever give her name or contact information to a stranger.

Reinforce her interest
in math and science,
both inside and
outside the classroom.

One of the most useful skills you can teach her is how to stand up for herself. Then she can stop anyone from picking on her.

Talk to her about drugs and alcohol early and often. You don't want her to learn this stuff from anybody else.

Never argue with her
mom in front of her.
As hard as it may be,
walk away.

Encourage her to trust her instincts, especially when a person or a place feels unsafe.

Remember,
society is teaching
her its values 24/7.
You need to be more
determined to teach
her yours.

Insist that she not wear makeup until she's in middle school.

Never permit her to
talk back rudely—to
you or to her mother.
Or anybody else,
for that matter.

Teach her patience, kindness, and tolerance. If you don't, many years from now you'll wish you had.

Display her artwork in your office. Why should all the good stuff go on the refrigerator?

Take her to the golf course with you. Give her a kid's club so she can whack balls around.

Encourage her
to compliment
others.

Eat breakfast with her. This will give her a reason to be at the table on time.

Think before
you speak.
Even when you
don't mean to, you
can end up hurting
her feelings.

Teach her that her actions speak louder than her words. Even if she's screaming her words.

Encourage her
to do good deeds
and not tell
anyone about
them.

Never laugh at
her dreams.

Impress upon
her the three Rs:
Respect for self.
Respect for others.
Responsibility for
all her actions.

Remind her to correct a mistake as soon as she realizes she's made one.

Encourage her
to spend time by
herself.

Teach her to read between the lines. Remember, though, that she will probably have a more natural ability for this than you do.

Share your
knowledge with her.
About your business.
About the stock market.
About quarterback
ratings.

Never let her forget
that you love her.
Even when you're
angry with her.

Remind her
never to interrupt
when she's being
flattered.

Take her out of town to somewhere she's never been at least once a year. This will develop her sense of adventure.

Don't miss a recital,
concert, play, or any
other performance
of hers. Not now.
Not ever.

Give her a picture
of you to put in
her first purse.
If you're lucky,
she'll always carry
a photo of you.

Encourage her
to be kind.
Even to the girl
nobody likes.

Make sure she can
reach you twenty-four
hours a day.

Tell her when
you're wrong.
And apologize.

$R$emember,
she needs a strong
self-image *before*
she becomes
an awkward teen.
A father's love can
make all the difference.

# The Mystery
# Years

Accept the fact that the loving, tender angel you've spent the last decade with may disappear sometimes. Don't worry—she'll return.

Remember,
teenage girls spend
hours in their rooms
doing something.
No man has ever really
figured out what that
something is.

Sometimes
(okay, many times),
she may not know
what she wants.
Your job is to help her
figure it out.

Once she begins
to develop
physically and
sexually, don't pull
away from her.

Insist she go to bed at a reasonable hour. Teenage girls need more sleep than babies do.

Have her hand over her cell phone at bedtime. This will force her to either study or sleep. It's also a preemptive strike against inappropriate texting.

Throw away the scales—weight gain during puberty is normal. Stress healthy eating, exercise, and plenty of sleep.

Tell her she looks beautiful in braces. Show her a photo of what you looked like in yours.

Friend her
on Facebook.
It's a handy way to
know what's going
on in her life.

Remind her that the most sacred thing shared by a father and daughter is trust.

Get to know all her friends. Middle school marks the zenith of peer influence.

Remember, by the time she turns thirteen, she'll have heard all about sex, drugs, alcohol, and violence from television, magazines, movies, friends, and the Internet. Hopefully she's already learned about them from you.

Lose the smartphone and spend time together as a family.

Remember, when you're dealing with a thirteen-year-old girl, for all intents and purposes you're dealing with a fruitcake.

Listen to the music she's listening to (and don't forget what your parents thought of what you listened to).

Talk to her often about decision making and sex. About peer pressure, about love, about romance, about God. You never know when it will be just the thing she needs to hear.

Teach her that
gossiping will eat
at her soul.

Never
underestimate
her intelligence.

Watch your language around her. Insist she watch hers.

Don't freak out when she says she hates her mom. (It's a mother-daughter thing. Just insist she show her mom respect.)

Give her household chores to accomplish and hold her accountable. This will help her keep in touch with family life.

Teach her not
to judge people
by the labels
they wear.

Review her homework with her nightly and drill her to help study for tests. This is an outstanding way to stay involved in her life.

Girls at this age can be uncomfortable stating what they really need. More often than not, she needs you to be a parent.

Adolescent girls congregate in shopping malls. Drive her there. Make sure she knows—and you know—who's bringing her home.

Don't put any more restrictions on your daughter's freedom than you would on a son of the same age and maturity level.

Accept the fact that girls squeal when they're happy or confused or excited or scared or because they just saw a certain boy in line.

She will get into spats
with her "best" friends.
She will have to deal
with mean girls.
You will feel—and be—
utterly powerless.

Tell her to believe
in true love,
just not in
middle school.

When she's particularly angry, sit down with her and have her try to describe what's going on. Remember, the longer you listen, the more you'll learn.

Monitor her TV viewing, movie watching, and Internet activity. Or else she just might believe she should be sexually active, dangerously thin, experimenting with drugs, and hanging out with rock stars.

Remember that most big sisters lord it over their little brothers. Remember, also, that most little brothers have ways of getting even.

Don't subscribe to magazines that exploit women. It makes a statement about how you view all women.

Play tennis or some other sport with her once a week. Even if you're a terrible player, it's a great way to spend time with her.

Facebook and YouTube and texting will all be part of her life. Make sure she is able to recognize and avoid dangerous or inappropriate possibilities.

If you don't approve of the way she looks before she goes out, send her back to her room to start over. Be gentle but firm.

There will be days
when you think you've
raised an alien.
Those are the same
days she feels she's
being raised by one.

No body piercing
below her ears—
this is where a dad
must take a stand.

The most stressful thing about her first school dance will be fitting a dozen girls into your car.

Girls can be emotional roller coasters and dads tend to be emotionally distant. She's part of your life; let it show.

Don't let her play you and her mother against each other.

There will be days when she'll think nothing you say to her is right. That's okay. You're the adult. Say what you feel needs to be said.

When she's looking
at the fashion models
in a magazine,
it's a good time to
discuss airbrushing,
advertising, and
marketing techniques.

Never call her names.
No matter how mad
you are. No matter
what she did. If you do,
she'll remember it for
the rest of her life.

Remember: Many girls look back on middle school as the worst time in their lives. Stay tuned in; stay involved.

Teach her to call you
if she's going to be five
minutes late or if she's
changing locations.
Always. That's why she
has a phone.

Be the one who takes her to her first rock concert. Take earplugs, though.

Teach her to read
the instructions.

Keep in mind that they only teach sex education in schools. It's your job to teach sex decision making.

Volunteer to drive her and her friends to the movies. Then just listen while they talk.

Don't hesitate to call her friend's parents if you know or suspect drinking, drug use, or sexual activity at their daughter's parties.
If it was you, you'd want to be informed.

Never tell
sexist jokes.
They will come
back to haunt
you.

Teach her to think before she speaks. But make sure you practice what you preach.

Impress upon her that there are direct correlations between studying and good grades, good grades and college, college and success.

Help her discover what she's passionate about, then help her pursue it.

Learn who her role models are. If they're just pop stars and fashion models, you have some work to do.

Face it—boys are now indispensable to her.

Understand that it's possible for a girl who has everything to be miserable sometimes.

Remember,
you can't always fix
all her problems.
In fact, your main job
is to teach *her* how to
fix her problems.

She may decide
to punish you by
not talking.
Enjoy the peace.

There will be times
when she will
blow you away with
her selflessness,
tenderness,
and gentleness.
This is the real her.

# Girls & Spirituality

The day she's born,
ask God to guide
you in all aspects of
raising her.

Talk about spiritual
matters at the dinner
table as much as you
talk about sports
or politics or her
allowance.

Drag her to church
or temple every week.
She may not share
your enthusiasm,
but after eighteen years,
there's a good chance the
message will sink in.

Forgive her when
she seeks forgiveness.
This is the best way
for her to learn to
forgive others.

Write her a short poem
or prayer that includes
her name and how much
you and her mother
and God love her.
Recite it to her every
night at prayer time.

Explain to her that
God doesn't speak
in code. She can figure
out what He wants
if she just stays in
contact with Him.

Teach her how to be moral in an age that bombards her with sexual imagery and innuendo.

Encourage her to join the youth group at her church or temple.

Stress to her
that one key to
happiness is never
to take everything
personally.

Ask her every now
and then about her
spiritual life. If she asks
you what you mean,
be prepared to have a
discussion with her.

Counsel her that finding an answer to a difficult problem can often be made much easier by asking, "What would please God?"

Teach her to pray for her enemies. This could possibly include a rotating cast of classmates and ex-boyfriends.

Teach her to treat her body as holy.

Encourage her
to look for the good
in everybody,
but to beware of evil
in the world.

Convince her that self-pity is a waste of time.

Help her understand that there's more to life than wearing the right jeans.

Teach her that sometimes God has other plans.

# Girls & Sports

Sign her up for a variety of sports when she's little. After a couple of seasons, let her decide which ones she'd like to continue.

Don't be the dad who takes his daughter's athletics too seriously. You'll miss some great times.

Her first soccer team may be called the Pansies. You may have to wear a T-shirt with pansies all over it. There are worse things.

**K**eep in mind that little
girls are not always
chasing the ball.
They're often running
simply because everyone
else is running.

Reassure her that
she will be okay
if she gets hurt.
(Reassure her
mother of this, too.)

When she's young, chances are she'll be better at sports than most boys. Don't let this go to your head. It's not genetics; it's child development.

The first rule
to lay down:
Grades always
come first.

**P**ractice basketball, softball, or soccer with her when you get home from work. She'll love playing with you. She might even beat you.

Teach her how to throw a curveball . . . and how to handle the curveballs life will throw at her.

Take her to college or professional women's sporting events. These athletes are real inspirations for young girls.

Go jogging with her.
Start when she's young,
so that when she
gets faster than you,
she'll still invite you
to join her.

Yes, girls today
play hockey.
You don't want to
be in the same rink
with them.

Don't think buying her soccer cleats is going to be any easier (or cheaper) than buying her other shoes.

Send her to sports camp. She'll come home bruised, exhausted, and possibly even bloodied—but also happy, fit, and a better athlete.

Don't forget,
competitive girls' sports
are no more played
by young ladies than
competitive boys' sports
are played by young
gentlemen.
It's rough out there.

Be prepared to
be amazed by her
accomplishments.

No matter how much
you're tempted,
don't yell at the refs
or insult the umpire.
You'll embarrass her
and look like an idiot.

Deal with the fact that if she's sixteen and still playing, you can't coach her. She's better than you will ever be.

Accept the fact that
she just may be a
terrible athlete. A lot of
gifted musicians and
mathematicians couldn't
hit a house with a ball
from five feet away.

You may feel the urge to paint your stomach and face with her team's colors. Curiously, this urge doesn't strike the fathers of boys.

Don't think that a boy
is the only thing that
can break her heart.
Losing a game can, too.

You may need to remind yourself that the other team isn't bigger. The other team isn't older. The other team wasn't just released from women's prison.

Remember,
athletics enhance
a girl's self-esteem,
increase confidence,
and improve scholastic
performance. As if she
needed an excuse.

# Show her how to lose with dignity.

Teach her how to
win gracefully.

# Girls & Money

Teach her that money cannot solve all ills.

Give her a piggy bank
when she's little.
She's never too young
to learn the value
of saving.

Provide her with opportunities to earn money, starting at an early age. Even a young child can clean her room, help fold and sort laundry, and water plants.

Send her on simple errands to the grocery store or drugstore, so she becomes comfortable handling money and learns the costs of basic items.

Give her a regular allowance. Raises and bonuses are possible, but should be earned.

Don't expect her to appreciate how hard you work to provide for her until she has to provide for herself.

She'll say she wants a handbag that's more expensive than her mother's. That's when you take her to the mall to fill out job applications.

Impress upon her
that there's honor
in a hard day's work.
And money.

Learn to say,
"We can't afford it."
She needs to learn to
say this, too.

# Show her how much to tip— and when.

Teach her not to buy anything with a credit card that she can't pay off each month. Explain how a $200 purse charged to a MasterCard could end up costing $400.

Instead of just telling
her to save money,
give her something to
save for: a smartphone,
a computer,
a new wardrobe.

# Teach her how to negotiate.

Remind her that
an independent
woman is someone
who's financially
independent.

If necessary, remind her that whining, crying, and begging won't gain her access to her father's wallet.

Show her how to read
the financial pages.
Tell her that serious
money is to be made by
those who understand
what they're reading.

Teach her to take her job seriously, no matter what the job is.

Discuss real-world costs. Like college tuition. Apartment rent. Utility bills. These things don't exist in her current world.

Explain to her that the greatest satisfaction of wealth is putting it to work to help others.

# Girls & Cars

You will have to teach her how to drive . . . without making her cry.

Let her drive you around. Sit there, look out the window, grit your teeth, and do not criticize her. This is how she'll gain confidence.

Realize her automobile insurance will be the price of a boat.

Make it very clear that you expect her to wear a seat belt. Even over her prom dress.

Lay down strict laws about drinking, texting, and talking on the phone while driving. Don't hesitate to enforce them.

Show her how to change a tire. She'll still call you at 1 a.m., but one night your cell phone may be on silent.

Make sure she learns
how to drive in the
rain, in the snow,
and on icy roads.
Stay at it until she can
drive in these conditions
with confidence.

Get her an
AAA card,
and make sure
she always carries
it with her.

Have a spare pair
of car keys made if
getting anywhere on
time is important to
you and your wife.

Before she sets off in a car by herself, remind her that her eyes must always be on the road, no matter how many times her phone beeps with text messages, calls, and Facebook postings.

When she's a new driver, place a limit on the number of friends who are allowed in the car at one time.

Remind her to use the GPS on her smartphone. Particularly the one with voice navigation.

Take a defensive driving class together. You'll both learn some valuable lessons about driving safely.

Don't buy the idea
that just because
she's a *she*,
she's automatically
a safe driver.

Remind yourself—
and your daughter—
that no teenager needs
a brand-new car.

You'll want her first car to be the biggest, most indestructible tank you can afford. While society might not sleep better because of this, you will.

Persuade her to buy gas when the fuel tank level falls to a quarter tank, not when the needle is buried and the car is riding on fumes.

Make it very clear that you won't take her side if she gets caught speeding, drinking, driving recklessly, or running a light. And that she will be carless until she's thirty.

Teach her that the most important thing to look for when buying a car is that it starts every morning.

# Girls & Boys

Odd-looking, strange-smelling boys will start showing up at your house. This is to be expected because adolescent boys are odd looking.
And strange smelling.

Let her see,
by the way you
treat your wife,
the way a man is
supposed to treat
a woman.

Tell her not to judge men by their looks or their money.

Teach her how to look a boy in the eye and say "No."

Do not tease her about boyfriends. She may not have one, and you might make her feel like she's supposed to.

Chaperone a school dance. You'll learn a lot about the boys in her life.

If she suddenly becomes a football fanatic even though she hates the game, you can be sure a boy is involved.

Teach her that
if she acts dumb
to attract boys,
she'll attract
dumb boys.

Don't assume that every boy who shows up at your house is a threat to your daughter's virginity.
He might just be her ticket to passing history.

Explain that there are dangerous boys as well as honorable ones, and how to tell the difference.

If a boy pulls up and honks for your daughter to come out, go out and have words with him. Explain that she answers to a doorbell, not a horn.

Remember,
it's a good thing
if the boys in her
life think you are
slightly unstable.

Tell her not to
feel overwhelmed
just because
an upperclassman
asks her out.

Do not follow her
on her first car date.
(You'll be tempted.)

Remind yourself that the alien creatures who show up at your front door looking for your daughter actually have parents.

Ask your daughter
and her date what their
plans are for the night.
If you don't like the plans,
help them make new
ones. Your daughter
will hate this.
It doesn't matter.

Make sure the evening ends with her date bringing her home, not taking her to another girl's house. Unless you really know and trust that family. And the boy.

Assure her that
her first boyfriend
won't be her last.
And to make
decisions
accordingly.

Know that she will not like it if you become better friends with her boyfriend than she is.

Wait up for her. Knowing Dad will be greeting her at the door has a very positive effect on the decision-making process.

Remember, every girl's heart gets broken. There's nothing you can do to fix it. Hunting down the boy won't help. On the other hand, she will also break a few hearts herself.

Understand that talking with your daughter about sex means you'll be having some of the hardest conversations ever. Keep in mind that they will also be some of the most important conversations you have.

If she starts moping at meals and barking at her family, and if she refuses to talk to one certain boy, you can be sure she's making his life miserable as well.

Teach her
to never confuse
abuse with love.
Violent behavior
does *not* mean that
he cares.

Stress that she's not to get into a car with a drunk boy, no matter how much she "loves" him. She should call you instead.

Make sure she knows she can call you at any time and you will come get her. This is why the cell phone was invented.

Tell her in no uncertain terms that if she texts an erotic picture of herself, the whole world could end up seeing it (including you). And that could change her life in a way she'll regret.

# Older Girls

Hug her before bedtime every night. Even when she's eighteen. It's important to remember what really matters.

Never forget, your influence is huge. The way you lead your life has a direct impact upon how successful she becomes in her own life.

Help her set goals. She needs something to shoot for.

Make sure she joins clubs or school organizations. She may say it's a waste of time and that none of her friends are doing it. But she'll get to know other goal-oriented kids. (Plus, it will look great on her college applications.)

Show her how to shake hands firmly.

Don't let her moods or anger push you away. She needs you now more than ever.

You have no power over how much shampoo, conditioner, skin cream, at-home hair color, mascara, eyeliner, lipstick, perfume, and body wash she will buy. Accept this and move on.

Assure her that she's a knockout. But remind her of all her other fabulous qualities, too.

Encourage her to compete—to run for the student council, to try out for the varsity team, to put something on the line.

But remember that competition can be absolutely ferocious, and losing will always be difficult and painful. If she doesn't succeed, comfort her—then put her back in the ring.

Talk to her often
about college.
About graduate school.
About careers.
About her dreams.

Be firm about maintaining family traditions. This will become more important to her than either of you can imagine.

When you're upset with her, don't bring up ancient history. Concentrate on the here and now.

Learn her language. When she says a date was "fine" or "okay," what is she really saying?

Remember,
fashion models are
thinner than 98 percent
of American women
and girls. Do not let her
believe she can diet and
exercise her way to
that look.

Stay out of the fights between her and her mother, unless you judge one or both as being completely irrational. Then venture in at your own risk.

Take long
walks with her.
If you just listen,
she'll eventually tell
you everything that's
on her mind.

Teach her not to take people for granted.

Set a strict curfew every year, based on her age and maturity level. Resign yourself to the fact that she will always complain about it—right up until she leaves for college.

# Never criticize her in front of her friends.

Teach her to avoid reckless people.

Remember to let her face the consequences of her actions. They are the best teachers. She doesn't learn anything if she's caught cheating or stealing and you come to her rescue.

Remember,
if her home life
is crazy, the rest of
her life will be, too.

# Teach her to respect herself.

Don't let her miss
school to get her hair
done for a dance.
It puts her priorities
out of order.

Remember,
you're her definition
of a man. If you drink
and smoke and use
drugs, chances are
the other men in her
life will, too.

She'll say you're
always lecturing her;
you'll say she
never listens.
You will both be right.

Remember:
The goal of being
a dad is to work
yourself out of
a job.

If she's embarrassed
by your car or her
car or her house,
she has some more
growing up to do.

Encourage her to volunteer. Community service is a great cure for teenage selfishness.

# Teach her to take the lead.

At some point she will decide that you need a complete, head-to-toe makeover. This will not make you look cool. It will make you look sixteen.

# Let her make mistakes.

Show her that
excuses aren't
necessary if she's
given it her all.

Understand that when she's fifteen and wearing a black dress, with her hair done and face made up, you will be very hesitant to let her leave the house.

Realize that you can't be everything to her.

Point out to her
that achievement
seems to follow
those who start
early and work late.

When it comes to parties, there's no such thing as too much information. Call her friends' parents and find out if they'll be present. If you suspect alcohol will be served, don't let her attend.

Don't think you've reached the perfect compromise by letting her and her friends drink in your home. All you're doing is teaching her to drink.

Help her learn to
be comfortable
with silence.

Teach her that
jealousy serves no
purpose other than
to make the jealous
person feel bad.

Remind her, continually, that she has the power to change the world.

Encourage her to be happy for other people's successes.

# Believe in her.

During those rare times when she actually wants to talk to you, turn the TV off and listen. You never know when this will happen again.

$T$each her
to stand up for
her decisions.
And to be willing
to change
her mind.

There will be times when you'd rather stick needles in your eyes than have a particular conversation with her. This is when you must act like a father.

Prepare for the day when you're not the most important man in her life.

Convince her not to be paralyzed by fear. Including fear of failure.

Visit colleges with her during her junior year. This is not the time to get emotional. This is the time for a reality check. Some colleges cost $50,000 or more a year, some $10,000. You love her—but what can you afford?

Have her finish all her applications by the summer before her senior year.

Don't let her choose a college because that's where her boyfriend is going.

Even when she's
a high school senior,
know where she's
going and who she'll
be with every night.

You'll notice that toward the end of her last semester of high school, her evenings will get started around the time you're tossing down your Metamucil.

Take her out to dinner, just the two of you. To one of your favorite places. Order food she's never tried.

Tell her the three keys to wisdom: not believing all you hear, not spending all you have, and not sleeping all you want. These will be difficult for her until she graduates from college.

Teach her that
great love and
great achievements
involve great risk.

# Compromise.

Let her know that
true happiness
comes from within.

Explain to her that not getting what you want is sometimes a stroke of luck.

Remind her that her character is her destiny.

Caution her against working *too* hard.

Assure her that she doesn't need any man to succeed or thrive.

Teach her not
to hold on to
anything too
tightly.

Explain to her that failure is an integral part of success, and that she must keep trying.

# Inspire her to never give up.

Have a look around
her room. Take a moment
to look at her photos,
her keepsakes.
These are her memories.
This was the childhood
you gave her.

Remember,
it will break your
heart when she
leaves for college.
But you will
survive.

Tell her she is the daughter you always dreamed about.

In the end,

Let her go.